Norma Huxtable's
EXMOOR EXPOSED

HALSGROVE

First published in Great Britain in 2007

British Library Cataloguing-in-Publication Data
A CIP record for this title is available from the British Library

ISBN 978 1 84114 688 1

HALSGROVE
Halsgrove House
Ryelands Industrial Estate
Bagley Road, Wellington
Somerset TA21 9PZ
Tel: 01823 653777
Fax: 01823 216796
email: sales@halsgrove.com
website: www.halsgrove.com

Printed and bound by Grafiche Flaminia, Italy

ot everyone loves Exmoor. Not everybody wants to be a hill-billy hitched together with baler cord in a place little changed, some say, from fifty years ago. In God's own country where the locals feel privileged to live, others claim they might be envious of our life-style, but it certainly wouldn't suit their needs. They smilingly admit money plays a part in their decision, and we tell them we're happy to assist anybody to redistribute their wealth. There's no disgrace in being poor, it's just the inconvenience of it.

After all it's the doing and the giving that counts in these parts, and doers and givers are always welcome, although not everybody feels fit to join in the social life at the end of their workday. Associations and fund raisers on Exmoor are more numerous than ticks on a sheep's back, and some new to these neighbourly get-togethers might offer a fiver in lieu of their presence. Whilst this could well cover the 'giving', ignoring the 'doing' very nearly amounts to a beheading offence. Everybody supports well nigh everything, and has to be seen to be supporting it. The foxhounds support the staghounds who support the foxhounds, livestock shows, the Air Ambulance and the church jumble sale, to name but a few.

Not everybody favours a classless society where we've all got our snouts in the same trough and it's not who you are, but what you are that counts; a place where your word is your bond and bills and receipts are replaced by verbal questions and sealed with a handshake. Anybody who breaches that bond might as well live in China. Exmoor is unforgiving.

Not everybody loves Exmoor enough to sacrifice their suburban Range Rover, with its tin of spray-on mud, for a temperamental tractor with terminal rust spattered with genuine sheeps' droppings. Nor do they fancy swopping a champagne flute for a mug of cider, or trendy theme pubs with exotic dancers for ones with antlers over the doors and, inside on the walls, portraits of huntsmen long since gone, and faded plaques that sternly insist, 'Play up and play the game.'

Not all ladies love Exmoor. Scrutinising the local newspaper for a chic beauty salon they can be forgiven for recoiling at the eye-catching advertisement that grabs them with the promise, 'Best prices paid for fat cows, plain cows, and maiden heifers.'

Not everybody who comes to Exmoor wants to sacrifice their vital statistics to trout, venison, rabbit, pheasant and clotted cream, nor do they savour exchanging their swimming pool for a sheep dip. Nor does every incoming young male have the same lustful desire for a muscled young woman with the obligatory whinny that can be heard three fields away. Neither does she crave somebody that might be unaware that sound travels faster than stags on the moor, but who is still not prepared to disclose the family scandals to save her time finding out.

Perhaps not everybody is prepared to love the brooding skies and the rain, and certainly not to embrace such an irritating old lot as us, the privileged few.

arvesting, ponders Farmer Fred, ain't just laid on for they holiday chaps who offers to lend a hand for a coupla hours of a summer's night, all dolled up in tight trousers with fancy labels on their backsides and check shirts like they come outa the boys chorus in Oklahoma. 'Tis more a long-term grind that commences in early spring with the sowing of seed, and winds up covering most months of the year. Countrymen would mostly agree with this logic but, although times have moved on, there is still some nostalgia for the pre-mechanisation era, the swish of the scythe and the neigh of the cart horses straining on their guide-ropes and the thud of hoofs upon earth. Back then the binder was an innovation in itself, replacing the reaping of corn by hand, although the sheaves still had to be 'stooked' upright by hand to dry in the sun and wind before being carried home by horse and cart.

The arrival of the tractor and the beginning of mechanisation replaced the horses, but the process remained much the same with the spring sowing commencing with Farmer driving the tractor and Missus working the attached corn drill, which demanded more guts than glamour. One farmer's wife, clinging to the dreaded drill, clanged it into gear only to be shot off down-hill into a steep goyle from which she emerged, painfully bruised, crawling up the field on her hands and knees. She was not invited back on the corn drill as her husband had noted rain clouds hovering and decided to take over her job himself, rather than waste time picking her up. He later excused her dismissal with an unworried 'I could see you wuz alright.'

Illustration by Avril Welsh

The arrival of combine harvesters eliminated, with one fell swoop, the all-day marathon of winter threshing, a nightmare for the womenfolk, commencing with a 7am breakfast for the threshing contractors, followed by the arrival of neighbouring farmers and their boy-chaps in time for forenoons at 11am with dinner sharp on 1pm and tea before they left for home to attend to their milking and livestock. Farmer Fred's missus recalls baking so gigantic a meat and potato pie for a threshing dinner that she had to call for reinforcements to extract it from the oven. Her Farmer/Husband/ Boss, ever resourceful, sprinted to the shippon, grabbed the cow shovel and returned to slide it under the pie dish, lifting it neatly from the oven. So hot was it, claimed Mrs Fred triumphantly, that bits of leftovers from the cows still clinging to the shovel actually started to cook along with the pie, the sizzling combination filling the kitchen with a quite unusual aroma, giving a whole new flavour to home baking.

Threshermen were accustomed to sumptuous food in their travels and anything less was referred to scathingly as a 'lettuce feast' and an incomer whose wife once (but only once) dished up macaroni cheese took the hint after hearing references to folks without teeth.

For all the hard work involved, these were thumping good get-togethers, now something of a lost era, a neighbour-liness that mechanisation has all but eliminated. Happily, one special occasion still remains, that of the harvest festival and the harvest supper afterwards. After all, as Farmer Fred reminds us, the best harvest is friendship. Coupled with meat and potato pie.

Farmer Fred reckons never to invest in anything that eats, or wants painting, which is a bit hard in a place like Exmoor where the main investment is sheep, who chomp their way through acres of greenery while the rams' chests are painted annually with a colourful substance called raddle. The very word has a bawdy ring to it, conjuring up visions of cartoon-like ewes at tupping-time, frisking their psychedelic behinds in the air after being 'raddled'. The EEC, naturally, recommends a change of practice involving pen and paper and complicated lambing forms, scrapping the farmers' hitherto simple formula of the ewes with red behinds lambing the last week in March, and those with blue behinds the first week in April.

As Exmoor men tend to live with their sheep, it is hardly surprising that they smell fresh from the sheep dip, which can have a fairly steadying effect on the womenfolk. Never-theless, in Farmer Fred's opinion, there's a woman for every sheep in the field. There's the ample sex-bomb who looks like a million dollars but never quite delivers the goods, producing one little squit-bang of a lamb each year that looks like it's crossed with a Pekinese. Then there's the sweetly shy one that never wants her undercarriage fiddled with, the bossy one who stands her ground like a Labour politician and the long-legged sport who sprints an assault course round the lambing shed like a four-minute miler. And, inevitably, the Glamorous Granny, with a fringe and dingly-danglies, that gulps down her Lonesome Trail mix and takes to the hills, never to reappear until dipping time, trailing a little mistake that looks as if Dad was a bit of rough that Granny picked up on Molland Common.

Farmer Fred fell in the sheep dip once, but survived after being dragged out by neighbours. He tells the tale to this day, recalling, 'They thought I wuz daid, but I wuz only fatally injured.'

Sheep are now, incredibly, becoming a fashionable accessory, no longer confined to Easter cards and calendars. They climb handles of little pottery jugs, peer from plastic pinnies, and meander in glorious colour across ladies' knitted bosoms. They look cuddly, pristine even, because you can't smell them, and no layman would dream that from Day One they are planning their own death. Preferably a dramatic one. A seizure at shearing-time sends everyone into a panic so maybe try a nice comfy snooze in the sun on one's back. That fools farmer nine times out of ten. Then the tenth time, the wind stops and it's 'Tee-hee, that'll cut your profit, Boss.' Drowning in the farm spring is as popular as it is spectacular, with the added bonus of giving the kitchen tap water a funny taste.

Whichever way out is selected, it finishes with a trip in the crowded knacker wagon to the kennels, and if the back doors fly open en route and a couple of bodies roll out and stop the traffic, so what!

Like Farmer Fred says, anybody who makes a living off sheep could teach they chaps up Westminster how to run the country. Profitably.

Come November and half the population outside any given village hall will be regaled by baritone voices drifting through the evening mist with such offerings as 'Mama's little baby loves shortening bread' followed by 'Home Cooking'. Inside, the scene is set for Widow Twankey's kitchen where the other half of the population is rehearsing for the annual Christmas pantomime. This involves casting, costumes and Mummies who insist 'Let's involve lots and lots of teeny children' but quail on finding they're expected to design and sew for twenty teenies dressed as chickens.

The biggest laughs, according to the cast, come at rehearsals, and such is the enthusiasm that some of the performers practise at home. One buxom lady, brimming with enthusiasm, persuaded the vicar to rehearse what had been a particularly stilted love scene in her home. 'Look at me,' she instructed. 'Look at me like I wuz a trifle.' The vicar squared his shoulders and advanced towards his lady, caught his foot on a chair leg and clutched at his partner to save himself, finishing up with both hands folded across her ample bosom. As though on cue, the door opened and a neighbour, known locally as 'News of the World', walked in. All three remained transfixed – end of scene, but with no merciful curtain to ring down.

Casting can often be open to criticism and whilst Prince Charming is usually a hard-riding, tough gal with tidy-sized thighs that crack thunderously when thwacked, the Princess has deceptively

little to do other than simper bewitchingly, which can be no mean task for a 40-plus leading lady in age and girth strapped into stays that are gutting her.

An all-male panto is a crowd puller and guarantees a line-up of hairy-chested chorus boys, but bib-and-brace overalls are out, along with silver wellies. Six big bruisers, planning to don fishnet tights with their tutus, were disconcerted when none could be found but the make-up artiste shaved their legs and painted on criss-cross fishnets which motivated the lads to strut their stuff to tumultuous applause. This was short-lived when the Good Fairy pulled the trigger on his wand expecting a puff of blue smoke and got instead an almighty explosion that left the audience diving for cover and the Fairy looking as if he'd been unloading a coal cart.

Every now and again one of the hunts puts on a panto where the dialogue is more basic than romantic and owes less to moon and June than the rutting season, and with an exchange of insults ranging from 'You be as stupid as Tom Yandle's hoss' to references to master's past indiscretions. Nevertheless, such is the razzamatazz of the theatre that a Dutch groom brought her parents over from Holland to cheer her on stage where she appeared as the back legs of the horse.

One huntsman, asked if he would take a couple of hounds to a rehearsal for a woodland scene, proudly let loose twenty whereupon they wrecked the trees and peed on the footlights, fusing the lot. The headline in the *Daily Mail* read 'Panto goes to the Dogs'. But it was still all right on the night!

A countryman tends to regard the sea rather like an old dog fox might sniff the demarcation line between boundaries. On the land side good solid earth to tread your boots in, whilst the other side can only offer acres of salt water with not a rabbit or a bit of greenery in sight. If you fall in the sea there's nort to get hold of, whereas on land you can wrestle with a pig and get covered in, well, whatever the pig is covered in, but at least you got something to hang on to.

Viewing the Bristol Channel from Dunkery is quite close enough to the sea for most folk and even then the travelling is better than arriving, with farmers scanning everybody else's fields and sheep and bullocks en route.

Howsoever, it can be unwise to pontificate about matters we know little about as when Farmer Fred decreed cruising was a crackpot holiday, with everybody dressing up like the Squire and all the time wishing they could be back home with their boots and braces stringed together with baler cord. Circumstances brought a change of opinion.

The next time Fred suggested to Missus that they might have a day up Cutcombe market she gave it a straight thumbs down in favour of a day out in Plymouth. For once Mrs Fred was determined and they duly arrived mid-morning in the city and she announced she was off to the shops. He opted to read a newspaper in the car, but this was Mrs Fred's day and she firmly pointed him towards the Hoe, telling him to explore and take a bit of interest for once.

Farmer Fred found he was enjoying his walk along the quayside when he came across a boat with folk climbing aboard. On an impulse he followed, thinking, as he said afterwards, why not, there's a first time for everything, even a trip on the dreaded sea. They cast off and almost at once his best cap blew overboard, but he didn't worry – he had another at home. The other passengers were a friendly crowd, passing the time of day and handing round a tray of whisky and sherry followed by plates of beef and ham sandwiches, then another tray of drinks. Fred took off his tie and unbuttoned his shirt to the waist like some of the young chaps. He felt carefree and reckless as they made for the open sea. He checked his pocket for his ticket money, but nobody collected. Another whisky came and went. This was serious stuff, thought Fred, but he had to find somebody to pay. Eventually he tackled a likely looking ticket collector to be told, 'But you've already paid, old son.'

'No I an't,' persisted Fred. 'I an't paid a penny.'

'Well then,' asked the man. 'What position do you hold, exactly?'

'I'm Farmer Fred from Exmoor. I just walked on.'

It turned out he had gatecrashed a works outing, but not to worry, they were delighted to welcome him aboard.

Three hours and several drinks later they disembarked and Fred hurried back to his car where Missus was pacing back and forth, on the point, she said, of sending for the police. He had lost his hat, he was tieless, his shirt unbuttoned and he was muttering, 'You'd bestway drive, Maid.'

She was disbelieving. 'You fool,' she said. 'Getting on a boat, you could've ended up in some foreign old place. No passport, not even a clean handkerchief you fool, you daft old beggar.'

'I've had a bootiful day,' he said.

If anything in the local newspaper causes our Exmoor farmer to clamp his tweed cap more firmly on his head and straighten his 'Eat British Beef T-shirt', it is to read of the threat that one or other of our local villages is to be twinned with a continental counterpart. He visualises his own personal patch of the moor being invaded by Hooray Henris fighting over the womenfolk and carrying on like old rams with a worm on the brain. But he fears not hefty, lederhosen-clad Germans sporting jaunty little hats with feathers, nor graceful, perfumed Italians with brooding eyes; our farmer defies competition in his striped braces and naily boots laced with baler cord. Not matching. That would be sinking to their level.

He fears not a swarthy brigand, pedigree unknown, wearing narrow trousers so tight that when he walks he squeaks, swirling a full length opera cloak lined with red satin and with a black sombrero tipped over a moustachioed face. He pictures him, sleek and sophisticated, crossing the farm yard with exaggerated strides, leaping lightly on to the muck heap in shiny patent shoes, to render a snatch from *Traviata*, then disappearing into the fowl house to sip a glass of red wine, raised to the nearest female – usually a hen – with the gallant toast, 'I drink to your beautiful eyes.'

None of this concerns our local man because he is only too aware that Exmoor women are unlikely to be swept off their welly boots by marauding foreigners; they are conditioned to a courtship conducted with more caution than verve. Introductions often take place on market day, with the three little words dearest to any farmer worthy of the name, 'How's your grass?' This little phrase can forge a lasting alliance between a countryman and a young lady who is regarded as not so much an object of desire as a possible stablemate. Then they unhurriedly winter, summer, and winter again before the wedding, providing, of course, she has the necessary qualifications for the job. Not too big a frame (they eat too much), a whinny that can be heard three fields away, the ability to dock a sheep with one hand and roll a fag with the other (for farmer, not her), and able to manage a bit of nursing for when himself gets cidered-up on Sheep Show day.

All this is alluring enough to countrywomen who are reared to respect masterful men, enhanced by the grim thought that if they leave it too late they could end up with an old dog fox.

On the other hand, if our man leaves it too late he might be forced to employ a housekeeper which is not only vaguely sinful, but costs a chap money. Farmer Fred always says that 'there's nort in this old love lark, 'tis all a question of h'economics and, above all, keep her at home and never let her see the other side of the fence.' Which brings us a whole lot closer to our Spanish counterparts and their favourite quote: 'Keep her at home with a broken leg.' Which makes our man appear manifestly benevolent. Viva our Exmoor man!

I wandered lonely as a cloud
That floats on high o'er vales and hills,
When all at once I saw a crowd,
A host, of golden daffodils.

A poem heralding spring that strikes a chord in the most stony hearted, that is other than practical minded farmers, one of whom was heard to observe that Wordsworth was very likely a chap with no proper work to do looking at good land gone to waste.

True enough, farmers are not big on flowers as village shops soon discover if they stock up on red roses for Valentine's day. There they all are, a week later, sad and wilted and unsold because the only blokes who carry home bunches of flowers have got to be big patsys that ought to know Missus would sooner have a lump of belly pork from the butcher next door.

As for actually growing flowers, well, that's gardening and gardening is a dirty old job. Farmers can shovel muck, stick their arms up cows' innards or take off perished lambs, but with gardening everything gets covered in black, cloying earth that sticks to the kitchen soap so that a chap's got to wash the soap before he can even wash his hands.

Exmoor men don't frighten easy, but it's no wonder that when Missus mentions gardening her spouse is likely to disappear in a cloud of dust and small stones. Getting him into the garden can take as much effort as dragging a clucking hen off a nest. Whereas he will plough acres of his fields and carefully sow and monitor his grass seedlings, his one purpose when faced with his lawn is to terminate its growth. And when it comes to machinery, there can be no bigger misnomer in the history of gardening than the Merry Tiller – an ill-treated implement that is kicked and sworn at annually and rarely presents the chuckling, merry jollity that its maker's name implies.

Inviting a few sheep into the garden can be useful enough to take the labour out of grass cutting, and they co-operate with their usual enthusiasm for tearing the place apart until the garden is planted and they are banished back to their field. In fact, they enjoy their work so much that they pay a return visit at dead of night and Farmer and Missus awake in the morning to the rhythmic chomping of contentedly grazing sheep finishing off the remains of their spring display.

A handful or two of fertiliser can work wonders in a garden, but the die-hards swear by the corpse of a dead sheep. It need not be exactly resident in the garden but it can still work its wonders on the other side of the hedge, in the vicinity, so to speak, whether buried or not, with the added bonus of promoting a fairish mushroom crop in that particular area.

Farmer Fred always follows what he calls the Maygrow Principle, broadcasting a mixture of seeds in the vague hope that they may grow. The rector, delivering Fred's church magazine, found him bad-temperedly digging his garden and intoned: 'It is indeed wonderful to see you helping God in His garden.'

'Huh,' said Farmer Fred. 'He didn't do a lot when He had it on his own.'

'See you at the harvest festival,' said the parson, hurrying on.

Most regular visitors to Exmoor must surely reflect that life among the natives could be even jollier if they only understood the language. They enjoy conforming to the rigours of the countryside, wearing baggy corduroys and sensible boots, tackling a cholesterol-defying diet, wind and rain and exhausting hikes/ gallops over the rough terrain. 'Windsor Park it ain't,' shrieked one such adventurer, clinging desperately to his hireling as it plunged at terrifying speed down the Devil's Punch Bowl.

Such stomach-churning experiences are recounted at night in the pub where the locals listen obligingly and comprehend. Our visitor, in spite of his 'ain't', enunciates in Queen's English. His problem arises when the locals reply, as he struggles to recognise a single word. They could be talking in Serbo-Croat. So, imagining that he is visiting a foreign country, he pronounces a few carefully rehearsed phrases. The locals then fire back a salvo with the velocity of a Kalashnikov, and the less he understands the louder they shout.

Here, as abroad, our visitor would welcome a simple phrase book, aware that a verbal cultural exchange could add a relaxing dimension to his action-packed holiday. In the absence of such a publication, a professor of Devon/Somerset dialects would be a benefit, and there's a whole assembly of professors in the pub every night (albeit with different day jobs). Our man decides to enlist as their pupil and listen, deliberately, heeding that in the country courtesies are observed and conversations commence with an enquiry as to one's health, 'How be 'ee?' A cautious 'Fair to middling' asserts that all is well, whilst 'I got a titch of the nadgers,' translates loosely into 'All is not well.'

He perceives that direct questioning is not a good idea, for a straight 'Yes' or 'No' does not come trippingly off the countryman's tongue; the tweed cap is removed and the head thoughtfully scratched until finally, 'Well, 'tis all according,' is released. 'Ort' and 'nort' are key words meaning 'something' and 'nothing', as in 'How is your wife?' 'Better than nort!' 'Howso-ever' denotes indecision whilst ten different answers are considered, and 'drekly' is a standby local tradesmen use, meaning they'll do your job next Christmas or next Easter, whichever comes last. Our student notes that 'Well done' is often used, covering praise for downing a pint of cider in one to falling in a nettle bed. It is voiced with five hundred different inflections.

He observes that colourfully descriptive words are voiced by his professors which relate more to their own (daytime) occupations than dialect in general. He is not sure that ladies would be impressed. To a cowman a fashionably slim lady is 'skintered', while to the equestrian a flirtatious filly is unflatteringly 'horsing'. A plumpish lady with 'a fine backside for sitting a clutch of heggs', scores a hit with the gamekeeper, with the accolade going to 'a proper maid'.

Glasses are filled and emptied in the quest for knowledge and the next morning the student reports a 'head like a thicket'. He braces himself for his next lesson.

Kissing don't last, cooking do' was often inscribed on wooden spoons presented to newly weds, the very tool suggesting a right old stir-up if things went awry in either department. Our menfolk might not themselves qualify as cooks but they expect their women to wash, cook and fettle and, as one worthy phrased it, to tell cow's dung from pudding.

With this in mind, it is now considered prudent, if not essential, to have a trial run before marriage. One countryman, although dazzled by his glamorous fiancée, was disappointed by her performance in the kitchen, particularly at breakfast. With Christmas looming, he decided on a subtle approach, wrapping her present in fancy paper and placing it under the tree. She picked it up and hugged it in anticipation before ripping it apart to reveal 3½ lbs of home-cured rashers. The cooking and the kissing were erased in one fell swoop.

If Missus goes away our countryman cannot be expected to fend for himself. He can manage without the kissing but not the cooking. When Farmer Fred's Missus flew off to Canada for three weeks visiting relatives, she left vast amounts of home-cooked food in the freezer, including various soups. Somehow, though, Fred never quite mastered the microwave, and although the soup heated it never liquidised and he ate it with a knife and fork. He claimed it might be more interesting if he found twenty-one women to cook one dinner apiece, followed by the threat: 'And then, Maid, you can stop away fer twenty-two nights 'cos I'll hev the best one back twice.'

Before she left, Mrs Fred endeavoured to cover every aspect of her husband's needs, even filling an empty Pimms bottle with vinegar from the cask and carefully re-labelling it. Various neighbours called to check on Farmer Fred, and one evening he decided to treat the ladies to a Pimms, not noticing the new label on the bottle. The ladies wrote a card to Mrs Fred, telling her they all got pickled on her husband's Pimms.

To our menfolk, handling a knife and fork can often prioritise over hygiene, and fast food can take on a whole new meaning without having to drive twenty miles to pick up a whalemeat take-away. Take, for example, two elderly bachelor brothers who sold poultry, which they chopped and eviscerated on their kitchen table, depositing the entrails in a tin bath underneath. Their meal merchant called and was hospitably pressed into sharing their fry-up. He noted their only concession to clearing the table was to spread a couple of sheets of newspaper over the deposits, then cover it with a tablecloth.

As the meal progressed, the detritus gradually soaked up through the paper and the cloth, introducing a mottled effect, whilst the innards in the tin bath underneath started to steam with a pungent vapour. The guest, whilst struggling to eat his sausages, managed to manoeuvre the bath away from his side of the table but it was footed back by one of his hosts in a silent, bizarre sort of pass-the-parcel game. Eventual escape to fresh air was bliss, pondering, no doubt, that there's no accounting for folks whose domestic arrangements vary a little from the norm.

'e never complained,' mourned a grieving wife at her husband's funeral. Probably not, and if he had taken to his bed she would quite likely have administered similar treatment to that given to comatose pigs and cattle: a smart thwack on the backside and a stentorian 'Giddey-up you mazed ha'peth'.

Farmers' wives are tough and can, if pressed, itemise an impressive string of their own ailments, ticking them off on one hand whilst thumping together a bran mash with the other. Rheumatics, ringworm, boils and bellyache (dismissed as wind), all registered under the umbrella of the Exmoor Nadgers, and inevitably concluding with 'But there, I can't complain'.

Farmer Fred reckons to be as resilient as most, frequently quoting the countryman's psalm: 'You got to farm like you'm going to live forever and live like you'm going to die tomorrow.' And, warming to his subject, 'Get to grips with a bit of fun, saddle up and gallop across the moor, fall off and pick up your teeth with your broken arm.'

Admirable as it is to plan ahead, nature can sometimes take over, as when Fred had an unplanned sting from a wasp and passed out in a field, coming round in a lovely warmth and opening his eyes to gaze up at a blue sky, the sun shining, the birds tweeting, and believing he had died and gone to heaven. He was brought back to the real world when he heard a cow bellowing beside him, causing him to leap to his feet like an old circus horse that starts to dance when it hears music. His resurrection could have been even more instantaneous if he had heard the peal of a hunting horn and realised the Staghounds had moved off without him.

This probably went down in the annals as one of Fred's standard days, simply because he only recognises two types of day, standard and fantastic. Another of his standard days was when he fell in the sheep dip and was dragged out, dripping, after marinading in disinfectant and green-ish slime, proclaiming forever afterwards: 'They thought I wuz daid, but I wuz only fatally injured.'

And Fred never complained. Which was unlike a city gent who moved into a nearby cottage and entertained hypochondria like a comedian entertaining an audience with deadpan mourn-ful patter. 'How are you to-day?' brought forth a mirthless, 'Well, I'm all right for the moment, but you never know what might happen', or a big wheezing cough and an anxious, 'Any idea how bird flu starts?' Farmer Fred's riposte to this was, eventually, brisk and practical. 'Sounds like you'm on the way out. Bestway git your Missus cracking on widow drill.'

'Widow drill? What's that, old boy?'

'Rodding the drains, cranking the generator. For after you'm gone. Her could give you a wreath first, then shoot you, and that way you'd both be happy.' Fred warmed to his theme. 'You could be like that old what's-his-name and have writ on your tombstone I TOLD YOU I DIDN'T FEEL

WELL.' There was no stopping Farmer. 'Your Missus could end up like that woman in the pub ordering drinks all round to celebrate burying her husband – not like he was like you, her said he never complained.'

Cow-punchers in the Wild West are said to commence their day shovelling down a breakfast of kick-arse cornflakes with milk poured over from a bottle labelled Jack Daniels. Our Exmoor menfolk consider a more healthy option with platefuls of fat bacon, eggs, fried bread and tetties. Some even add a couple of lamb chops. After all, they reason, Grandad stayed an old dog fox with an eye for the vixens until he was ninety-six, feeding on a daily diet of fat bacon from the cradle to the grave. Generally, breakfast appetites fade only if Missus is laid up and Farmer is left to his own resources; one even admitted to trimming his intake to a pint of cider and a cream cracker.

Years agone 'forenoons', alias elevenses, were a popular mid-morning break, usually tea and cake, but that was before farmers and their wives worried about looking like their own pigs wearing jumpers. Now the menfolk are good and ready for their dinner at one o'clock sharp. While the rest of the world lunches, countryfolk sit round kitchen tables to gravy dinners, roasts and stews and cow pie, presided over by Missus in her floral pinny. Her job is to dish up dinner on time; there's no question of her not being present to wait on the menfolk, but is never included in their conversation, other than 'Over this way, Maid, with the tetties.'

Farmer, sitting at the head of the table, eats as much as he can for a man with only one mouth, siphoning in food like a tractor taking on fuel, firmly believing that no decision, no matter how piddling, should ever be made on an empty stomach. Ample desserts, smothered in cream, are expertly dealt with before the diners file out, fortified, ready to confront any dissenters from marauding tax men to anti-country sports folk who have possibly lunched less courageously on half a wholemeal sandwich filled with chopped parsley and washed down with turnip juice. Missus surveys the dishes and has a fleeting, unworthy thought, that, as far as she is concerned, a man at the sink could be worth two in the yard. Although countrymen are hardly classed as fussy eaters, a few taboos from Grandad's day still prevail. Blackberries are never picked after 29 September when the devil spits on them; wild geese are so tough that they should be cooked with a brick in the oven so that the goose can be thrown out and the brick sliced and eaten. Mutton loses its appeal at lambing time and a wobbly jelly at tea can effect a mild stomach upheaval.

The eating habits of immigrants to Exmoor are observed and often learnt from, although at times emphasising the culture gap between town and country. One lady, with aristocratic leanings, alternated between Nouvelle Cuisine, with platefuls of tastefully arranged flower petals covering minuscule grams of fish, to Wally Wallaby's Whopping Burgers. Her afternoon teas scorned scones and cream in favour of cucumber sandwiches with the crusts cut off which, she explained, was no less than her friends would expect. 'Whaffor?' Farmer Fred wanted to know. 'Ain't they got no teeth?' 'Of course they've got teeth,' she replied indignantly. 'The Queen always has the crusts cut off her cucumber sandwiches.' She swept off, leaving Farmer Fred scratching his head, striving to piece together the connection. 'They sort of wimmen,' he says, 'got a job to tell cows' dung from pudden. What they wants is a coupla rashers o' fat bacon.'

Countrymen are rarely seen to admire dead stock (i.e. cars) in the way they admire live stock (a prize bullock or a weight-carrying hunter). For them a dual-purpose vehicle is considered way above a gung-ho model – a bit like Missus, Exmoor mare rather than ornamental show pony. A salesman spraying a car with the new yummy leather smell would induce the simply-must-have in a farmer on a level with a three-legged sheep. If it were not for MOTs, anything with wheels would suit most country folk. One man used to teeter frighteningly across Exmoor in an ancient three-wheeler, his only doubts revealed by the sealed envelope he left on his mantelpiece at home instructing 'To be opened in the event of death'.

Those who remember that fine old Exmoor character, Dudley Down, could never forget his Mini which went dead slow when he was watching a hunt or jet-propelled with the ignition switched off when he cruised for free downhill. He also tended to save on roundabouts by cutting across on the right, his philosophy being 'They'll see me coming'. And he never set off anywhere without packing what he called his indispensables – a pair of red silk pyjamas and a pot of Gentleman's Relish.

Some countrymen never make the driving test or even pay for proper tuition, taking lessons from friends which they look on as a bit of a lark. One learner managed to talk his neighbour into accompanying him across the moor most evenings, stopping off into a pub until closing time, then, with the learner driver refreshed, driving home. This went happily on until one foggy night

when he careered off the road and on to the moorland, shouting, 'Whoa, come back you beggar'. The instructor, previously not a nervous man, resigned there and then, saying he'd sooner go back to syrup of figs than give any more lessons. A test was never taken.

Farmer Fred always believed in mixing business with pleasure and delighted Missus when he ordered her to pack up a picnic and said they would have a day out, forgetting to mention that they would be sharing their day with their nanny goat that Fred bundled into the back of their van. The three of them set off for the Valley of Rocks where they tethered the nanny on a grassy patch and enjoyed their picnic whilst the resident billy obligingly provided a service for free. Farmer called it killing two birds with one stone – he'd saved a tenner on a stud fee and kept Missus quiet with a day out.

Nevertheless, Farmer Fred admitted to a liking for what he called charabanc trips (men only). Once, he recalled, they went to Cornwall and picked up a dead shark on the shingle and loaded it on their coach for a souvenir. On the drive home some of the Men Only began to feel unwell and traced it to the shark being somewhat less than fresh. Spotting a garden with a pond in it they off-loaded their nauseating souvenir, but too late to stop the fishy stench pervading the coach for infinity.

Mrs Fred told her husband that she had often wondered what the Men Only trippers got up to on their outings. 'Next time you go off to Cornwall,' she said. 'You can go in the car and' – threateningly – 'I'll go with you.' 'Don't talk so daft, Maid,' said Farmer. 'Us'd never git a shark in a car...'

f Missus ever mentions the word holiday, our Exmoor man disappears faster than a rat up a drainpipe. Countrymen don't rate holidays, they are comfortable working the land they know and love; they don't want shops, wine bars, discos, anywhere without livestock or, the ultimate horror, beaches. Ten to one any countryman bulldozed by wife and family into visiting a beach will sit there forlornly in his best clothes and clip-on braces with the *Western Morning News* spread across his head muttering, 'How soon can us go home?'

Holidaying on another farm can be almost acceptable as it can turn into more of a working holiday. One Exmoor man, booked in to a farm in Dorset, castrated all their pigs and then spent a day riding their cabbage planter.

A trip to the Fells can be quite popular as is a men-only visit to Scotland, incorporating tours of the distilleries, from which the participants return looking a shade paler than when they left.

However, failing a short break, it is likely that Missus will settle for a day trip out. When Farmer senses this looming he tends to get in first with 'Right, Maid, us'll have a day up Taunton market.' Not Exeter. Exeter is considered to be a bit smart, sophisticated even, and, as one over-ruled farmer put it, only useful for two things – one's to have a haircut and the other's to get drunk. Point-to-points meet with more approval as do farm sales and a day's hunting.

For those of us whose geography does not extend beyond Blackmoor Gate, any travelling can be regarded as an expensive luxury. Our menfolk have been heard to pontificate that a week's holiday spent sleeping in bed works out a sight cheaper, saving on car usage, electricity and food (you don't get so hungry). Wives are not wildly enthusiastic over such savings and one tells of how she seized the initiative to resuscitate honeymoon magic by booking herself and her Farmer/Husband/Boss into a hotel for the weekend, to include a Saturday night dance. The music strummed romantically, couples whirled and twirled, the wife sipped a Babycham while her partner downed a couple of pints of his usual superphosphate to get in dancing mode. Then, reluctantly, he took to the floor with as much enthusiasm as a trailer load of King Edwards. Meanwhile, upstairs, their bed was turned back with the husband's pyjamas artfully arranged displaying a thrifty patch with an old flour bag printed THIS WAY UP.

Now that line-dancing has hit Exmoor the menfolk seem relieved that their women can enjoy dancing weekends without them which is a definite plus, but a minus is that some women are never satisfied, and their thoughts are even straying to holidays abroad. Farmer Fred reckons you want to keep clear of that old lot for 'tis all rum, bum and gramophone records and the next day all you get is a thick head and rumbling guts because nobody eats proper food, just cauch with a spoonful of rice that they don't even put jam on. 'Tis healthier (and cheaper) to go for a good gallop across Exmoor and then go home to a proper dinner …with tetties.

ong before unisex garments there was Lord Carnarvon's livery consisting of two corn bags – one hooked round the shoulders, the other round the waist. Not so much a fashion statement by both gents and ladies but allowing freedom of movement and worn to keep out the worst of the Exmoor weather.

What folk wore underneath was open to speculation, although interlock loomed largely in the lingerie line-up. Years agone countryfolk dressed thoughtfully for the winter with red flannel and a covering of goose fat smothered over brown paper. This was flattened on to chests where it stayed until spring, attached to the same stripey, collarless shirt, the principle being that no matter how anybody looked or smelled, warmth was there to stay.

Bathing was a no-no and few farmhouses had bathrooms upstairs. ('It ain't natural fer water to travel h'upwards,' voiced one farmer, to general approval). In any case, bathing was considered unhealthy, washing away the natural oils that keep a chap warm, with one old-timer admitting he had not had a bath for sixty years, adding defiantly, 'And I'm lily white.'

As with horses, it has always been thought best to 'put warmth in the manger'; feeding winter fodder in the form of rib-sticking food, pork fat and pickled onions being particularly recommended. One old character was actually known as Fat Bacon Charlie, living well into his eighties on this chosen diet. He was also known to favour a tidy drop of spirit poured over his breakfast porridge, followed by a roll-up. He was, however, said to stop short of smothering his naked body in peanut butter, another fancied remedy for keeping out cold.

Back in the days when a farmer could just about afford a labourer, it was vital, even on a meagre wage, to keep them working. Farmer Fred says he can recall his father on rainy days strapping a sheet of galvanized on to the workman's back so that it provided a little roof over his head and he was able to go out in the fields hedging. The young Fred fared little better, his father feeding him a plate of red meat twice daily, followed by a boot up the backside to get best results.

'Us be all too softy now,' says Fred, himself included. Only last autumn he bought a bag of rat poison that included a free pair of gloves. 'I only bought thik particular bag 'cos of they free gloves,' bemoaned Fred. 'And then I went all soft and giv'd 'em to Missus fer Christmas. Her was some delighted, but there's me still wearing odd socks on me hands. Gone soft in the head, I have.'

Come the spring and heigh ho, scrubbing up commences, albeit with some caution, a layer at a time. Red flannel, stays, interlock replaced with aertex, the peanut butter swilled and even Missus' winter hat abolished, which somehow by spring attains the flattened contours of a dead hen.

Adjusting to spring can be something of a wrench, even in this modern age and ne'er cast a clout 'til May is out still figures in many a mind. A lady, invited to a private pool for a swim took the plunge wearing winter tights underneath her costume. The spectators were divided between warmth and modesty! But what the heck – this is Exmoor, not *Vogue* magazine.

Tradition has it that there are three maxims which ring a bell for every Exmoor man: *Of course I'll love you the same in the morning. We are sending a man from the Ministry to help you. That is the finest racehorse I've ever seen.*

Whilst the first threat might provoke a man-of-the-world 'That's a load of bull!' and the second motivate Farmer into a passing kick at the pig bucket, the third could bring about a lecture on the merits of racehorses, racecourses, and even include the tale of the Man from the Ministry who turned up at an Exmoor farm one fine day to count sheep.

The farmer was geared up for the inspector with a couple of fairish-looking horses saddled up, hoping that his thoughtfulness in saving the subsidy man's feet the lengthy trek to the field might be taken into consideration should he have mis-claimed on one or two sheep. The elected rider was doubtful: he had not ridden for years, but what the heck. The two old nags were standing there in the sun quietly nodding off, it was too good an offer to pass up. He climbed aboard the chestnut and he, with Farmer on the grey, gently set off for the sheep field. As soon as they hit the big field and Farmer yelled, 'Hold tight' he realised his folly. The two horses took off, racing neck and neck across the ten-acre field, sheep charging in every direction. Eventually managing to pull up, Farmer was unstinting in his praise for the new jockey. 'You done a proper job, Sir,' he enthused, leaning across to thwack the Man from the Ministry between the shoulder blades. 'These two be entered fer Newton Abbot next week. Might be worth a bet.'

Although an enthusiastic racegoer, Farmer Fred never actually owned a racehorse, strictly adhering to his own advice that if you want to do somebody a bad turn you give them a racehorse. Owner's expense is whacking, with passports, shoes, transport, trainers, jockeys and even après-race celebrations should the horse make even a lowly third in the frame, be it in the Gold Cup room at Cheltenham or the Tote bar at Taunton (a shed in the middle of the racecourse).

Trainers, for years a male preserve, have now been infiltrated by tough ladies half expected to spit tobacco juice and sneeze snuff when in fact it's a whole new glamour area. The beautiful, independent toughies might well have a front like a duchess and legs like shovel sticks, but can be casual to the point of disdain with any man that's not up to scratch after a plate of red meat, followed by a kick up the backside if he's five minutes late mucking out in the morning.

One lady trainer was actually proposed to in the unsaddling enclosure by a euphoric winning owner and they married in a blaze of publicity, their union blessed with three sons named Kempton, Sandown and Bangor.

Mrs Fred never shares her husband's enthusiasm for racing, declaring no interest in what she calls sax and saddle soap. She'd sooner stop home and skin a rabbit, but Fred always rings her at the end of a winning day, setting his call to music with 'We're in the money, tra-la.'

Optimism is the name of the game, but there's a judgement somewhere when a well-known bookie, asked if he had a red-hot tip, replied: 'Never bet!'

The winter weather on Exmoor often merges into a pot-pourri of cloud, drizzle and fog, but thankfully the mood rarely matches the climate. Far from retreating behind closed doors Exmoor folk go 'urnabout', or 'rinabout' if you're North Devonian. Parties, card schools and slide shows unfailingly draw the revellers, every event followed by a gargantuan supper, the belief being that no nocturnal event should be concluded on an empty stomach.

This socialising was cruelly curtailed one winter with the foot and mouth disease upsetting the whole country scene and folk being shut off from the outside world. On the whist drive circuit, old friends, and even old adversaries, missed meeting up several times a week. One player, now joyfully back in circulation, claims that hearing the first shout of 'hearts is trumps' very nearly ties with the huntsman blowing 'Gone Away' in his list of favourite things. Now, once again, the moors are alive with carloads of card players in search of whist drives. They select their venue before they set off from their warm, cosy homes, but it's hit or miss whether they ever reach their selected village hall in the fog. Their crammed-in passengers all shout different directions though, with the number of whist drives on any one night, any hall will do, even if they have to sit freezing in their overcoats and woolly hats.

Once inside, the evening commences with an exchange of friendly greetings, but whilst some play with the traditional poker face, others try gamesmanship, scooping up their cards with a despairing aside – 'This hand's as black as a cow's innards' – aware that bull often baffles brains. At table number ten Granny coughs loudly and everybody in the hall is wise to it – Granny's got the ace of trumps, the pre-arranged cough being the secret signal to her partner.

A twelve-year old shuffles the pack like a New Orleans card sharp and a newcomer marvelling at such skill, is told matter-of-factly by the young player, 'Well, I've had twelve years of experience!' There are two players over, so this means sitting out for one deal at a 'flirtation table', where they each take a generous eight points. The flirtation is not of the lonely-hearts type, the conversation likely to be revolving round udder cream and worm drench.

Neighbourliness and old world courtesy may take a downturn in the second half when a couple of points can be the difference between taking home a full-blown chicken dinner or a tin of super-saver baked beans. Here a hesitant player can earn a scornful rebuke for ruining a partner's hand by placing a low card instead of a high one. 'Tis no good sending a boy to do a man's work!'

Prizes abound, even for the lowest score there is what used to be called the booby, now termed more kindly, the consolation prize, upgraded, some say, by human rights campaigners refusing to acknowledge the degrading 'booby'.

As they all pile into their transport home for some it's been a 'standard' night, for others 'fantastic'. Those are the only sorts of night you get at whist – there's no such thing as a bad one.

Politicians, so Exmoor chaps say, be a lot like women; you got to summer 'em, winter 'em, and summer 'em again before making up your mind to a four-year stretch or even a lifetime, depending on the candidate, whether 'tis voting or marrying.

Even more worrying could be a combination of the two, like a lady candidate with ambition to become Chancellor turning out too tight-fisted to knit a sparrow a pair of leggings or, worse still, a Caring Candidate, dedicated to outing the demon drink from farmers' lifestyle.

A general rule might be it's no matter how they look as long as they can swear, roll a fag and down a pint of cyder, disregarding that politicians' minds are thought to be on loftier matters. Howsoever, it's not who you are but what you are that counts, particularly with Exmoor being a place where bull baffles brains.

Glib, articulate canvassers are a must and essentially they need to be local and able to recognise the bundle of rags in a farmyard as their target voter. Knowledgeable interest must be displayed and no wondering aloud why farmers always site their gates in the muddiest part of the field. A quick time of day and a passing 'I trust I may have your vote', would be condemning an etiquette to be observed by both participants.

A canvasser tackling Farmer Fred had to wait whilst Farmer leant back against the barn door, using it as a scratching post for between his shoulder blades, then thoughtfully and painstakingly filled his pipe with baccy before uttering a single word. Hardly had they commenced when Mrs Fred trudged past pushing a steaming wheelbarrow of dung towards the muck heap, compelling her Farmer/Husband/ Boss to mildly rebuke: 'Next time, Maid, kick over they mole hills as you go.'

'How can I,' she wailed. 'I shall upend me load.'

'Ought to hey bin a politician herself, that one,' grumbled Farmer Fred. 'Always contrary and shouting the ruddy odds.' Then turning to the canvasser: 'What ratass party be you from? Only sensible policies I ever heard come from screamin' Lord Sutch with pickled onion trees, booze-filled lakes and, in particular, stronger drink and wider roads. Now, my lad, beat that.'

Village halls can offer marginally more comfort than draughty farmyards or rain-swept cattle markets, but venues whatever are meat and drink to aspiring politicians. They have no choice, they're in it with one foot in a cow pat and the other in a pile of sheep droppings, and, as one candidate was heard to nervously observe: 'Countryfolk are all very well spread out a bit – but not so good all in a heap.' Neither do they need hecklers when Granny's in the front row loudly inter-rupting: 'What's he say, what's he say.' Then a voice from the back: 'Give us a kiss, I don't sick easy!'

Meetings often finish on a lively note with blasts from hunting horns which can rate somewhere between cheers and boos, depending on the call and finishing with either Gone Away or Accounted For as the candidate seeks the safety of the Battle Bus, mouthing a few unheard words which might be 'I trust I may have your votes?' … Or might not!

t is unlikely that any revellers cheering the prize-winning ceremony of Miss Dung Heap 1987 has ever forgotten it. The winner was a beefy farmer sporting a bubbly ginger wig and squeezed into his mother's old evening dress, his naily boots peeping from under the figure-hugging skirt. Six similarly attired losers jeered the judge's verdict, the one in a bonnet with red ribbons mouthing RATBAG at the winner already slurping from his first-prize bottle of whisky. As this was all of fifteen years ago the phrase 'men in drag' summed it up, conjuring up visions of Les Dawson lookalike guys in skirts and stays parodying hairy-chested women straight out of the sheep-dip.

Nowadays, according to the media, this is no longer a matter for ribaldry, as it is important for men to be (quote) 'in touch with their feminine side', turning HE into SHE at the flick of a dominant wife's little finger, and even strutting their stuff in the street wearing her clothes ('underwear and all, dearie!'). This new man is rumoured to pick at a wholemeal sandwich filled with finely chopped parsley for his lunch, and would even throw that up at the sight of our old knackerman skinning dead sheep, then wiping his knife on the backside of his breeches before slicing up his fat bacon sandwiches.

Paradoxically, the Exmoor male is often quite ready to concede that his Missus has a tough, even masculine side, which he takes for granted. Our men are butch enough never to feel emasculated, the womenfolk being allowed, nay even expected, to hump bales and churns, just so long as they remember their place and never, ever over-reach themselves and cross that thin dividing line between helping and interfering.

One wife is known, by mutual agreement with her Farmer/Husband/Boss, to be first out of bed every morning, racing out to milk the house cow and feed the calves and chickens before returning indoors to find her man seated on the old kitchen settle awaiting his breakfast. The conversation, which he occasionally recounts in the pub, never varies.

'Cup of tay, Maid.'

She hustles to the Rayburn, sets the kettle on, then carries him his tea.

'Bit of toast, Maid.'

Three rounds of toast are thickly buttered and carried to Farmer.

Then, finally, 'Boots, Maid.'

She picks up the naily boots and exchanges them for slippers. Farmer is ready for work. He is philosophical over his delayed arrival downstairs in the morning. ''Taint the time you gits up, 'tis what you do afterwards. You see, m'dears, if the good Lord had intended I got up in the morning He'd have giv'd me the strength to do it. But He hain't. He've giv'd it to her instead.'

It seems likely that our sarong-clad New Man, raising his champagne glass with his be-jewelled fingers is by now firmly in touch with his feminine side. Meanwhile, unfazed because it's cocktail time in the Met Bar, our Exmoor Man is diving into his poacher's pocket for a muddied hip flask. It's what Farmer Fred might call a black dog for a monkey.

'eep her at home with a broken leg' runs an old Spanish proverb. Our Exmoor man scorns what he calls a load of old bull when all they foreign chaps got to do is to remind Missus that summer's arrived and it's Bank Holiday and the usual Boys' Day Out.

Farmer Fred says Missus calls it summer madness and he reckons she got that from some old film that turns up on telly every Bank Holiday. Mrs Fred fires back saying Fred's summer madness commences at Easter when he spends every spare minute trekking the fields and coverts searching for stags' antlers, finally arriving home looking like he's had a month up the Amazon. Later there will be antler competitions, every entrant a potential winner.

Next on Farmer's Bank Holiday list is a Steam Engine Rally with active participation limited to cups of tea and doughnuts. A more energetic favourite for the Boys' Day Out is a tug-o'-war involving all the hefties with big boots and Fred praying it won't bring on a coronary.

Wives are sometimes invited when there's a country fair, mainly if feeding is involved. One of the most memorable sights ever witnessed on Exmoor was a gunge bath for charity. It comprised an old fashioned tin bath with a volunteer (the only one) squeezed into it properly dressed in check shirt and drill trousers. He was a hefty seventeen-stone huntsman and the crowd was invited to purchase buckets of slops for £1 which they then upended over his head – tea leaves,

bacon rinds, old tomatoes, rotting fruit, curdled milk, stale doughnuts, in his hair, down his sodden shirt, inside the bath, outside the bath. It was a fundraiser the like of which had never been seen before – or since. Eventually the volunteer was prised from his gunge to an ovation of the sort accorded to the London Marathon winner. The cheering continued until he was out of sight on his long walk home where Missus was waiting to give him a good rub down with Jeyes Fluid.

A lot of countrymen fancy ferret racing on a day out, or, come to that, anything at all to do with ferrets. A ferret can be as much a part of a family as a dog or cat. Many folk will recall the old gravedigger who made a picnic of the digging, taking along his missus and kids and the family ferret. Years agone ferret owners wore breeches and gaiters, knowing that ferrets could develop a sudden turn of speed that shot them up inside a trouser leg. Even so, it is still considered quite sporting by some to deliberately shove a ferret down their trousers for bets, even with the threat of Accident and Emergency looming and any injuries kept secret from Missus.

Meanwhile, back home, there's Mrs Fred living the old *Summer Madness* yet again on telly, all set in Venice, no ferrets, no gunge bath, just Katherine Hepburn being romanced by a dark-eyed, hand-kissing Italian. He buys her a gardenia and as the orchestra dies away Mrs Fred dabs at her eyes, reaches for her boots and bucket and floats down the yard to milk the cow with sore titties...

lot of town-dwelling high fliers, swept up in their careers of high finance, promotions and paid holidays, might think, on one of their whistle-stop weekends in the country, that there is a gentler theme to life, more come-a-day go-a-day, than whizz-bang-wallop, here comes a zillion pound take-over.

Farmer Fred, in the rural setting of his own Exmoor empire, couldn't agree more wholeheartedly, that living is all a matter of h'economics, but, then again, there's no disgrace in being poor, 'tis just the inconvenience of it. As for paid holidays, they be all very well if a chap's got nort better to do whereas hard work and a bit of self promotion does nobody any harm. Only last week odd-job man Fat Bacon Charlie was pushing Fred to demolish and re-build a couple of old tin pigs' shelters. Although Farmer was doubtful of Charlie's ability to handle anything more than a pint pot, he was impressed by the sales promotion when he claimed: 'Put it this way, Squire, just you say the word and I can dismantle Buckingham Palace, brick by brick, and re-build it, queen and all, in the Gobi desert.' Fred liked the reference to royalty in connection with his pigs' houses but was astute enough to realise the palace was hypothetical whilst his boots were there and then stuck firmly in the mire of practicality. Thumbs in braces, he enquired in his country business-man-of the-year tone: 'You got any more loss-making enterprises, then?'

It is likely that countryside folk match their city counterparts by being super efficient in their respective departments, with the farmers advising never to invest money in anything that eats or

wants painting, whilst the manufacturer waxes enthusiastic over 127 different types of supermarket shelving. Which does not apply to the freezer department. Quite. This statistic totally eludes Farmer Fred whose carpentry was confined to once knocking up a wheelbarrow 'uta me head'.

Away from the top end of the tycoons, but still head of their own department (usually only of one) is the working sheep dog and the farm cat employed to mouse in the feed shed.

Whilst in the city, work incentives are offered in the form of bonuses, in the country it is not considered a good career move if Missus opts out of Cutcombe sheep market and swops her welly boots for comfy shoes and a day at the sales. Bonuses in the country are limited to a bit of bartering, like a tame lamb for a joint of brisket, or a day out staghunting for a bottle or so of Grouse. Which brings us to the Wild Life Department where the rutting season is work to be taken seriously by the Red Deer stags. Because sound travels faster than light on Exmoor, conversations are overheard and faithfully reported, in every department, unmatched by any city slicker. Like the old stag and the young one standing together on Molland Common, looking lasciviously down the valley at a herd of hinds. 'Yo-ho, 'yelped the youngster. 'Let's charge down there, Matey, and grab all us can afore they all urn off.'

'Hold hard a bit,' restrained the knowing old boy. 'Us'll creep down and take the lot.' Better than any city bonus.

eighbours come in three sizes, interested, inquisitive and just plain curious. Which is an indication that if you want to keep a low profile the last place you should move to is the countryside. Those with a Past or criminals on the run may, of necessity, be all clammed up, and back where they came from they may have robbed banks, planned routes for getaway cars, hired henchmen and escaped with the swag, but they are making a big mistake if they plan to lie low in a country cottage. Life is busy in the countryside and they are undoubtedly embarrassed by neighbours' invitations to join in short mat bowling, a village knit-in and the Silver Threads club (over sixties only). They are unfamiliar with the country code of 'tell us your business and 'twill save a lot of time finding out'. They therefore have to balance reticence without appearing to reject neighbours with a curt 'I just wanna be on me own' as did one lady who was noted paying for every purchase in the local shops with fifty pound notes, arousing even more suspicion. Hers was a short stay before she moved back to the anonymity of London where, it is likely, neighbours take far less notice, in fact one immigrant was heard to say they never had neighbours, just people who lived next door.

In the countryside they are not always just next door, but far more scattered, although still referred to as 'neighbours', even if they live on the other side of the moor. Newcomers are often surprised to find, once they are accepted, that they qualify for the little country offerings that are casually tossed on their kitchen table; a rabbit, a fine trout (or two), a brace of pheasants. No payment is ever accepted, nor, according to the country code, should ever be proffered. Howsoever, neighbours are likely to appear with their gifts at any ungiven time, as Farmer Fred did one afternoon at a newcomer's cottage, bearing a cabbage from his garden. He had previously heard the new folk discussing knowledgeably the merits of fresh food, and a cabbage was the best contribution he was able to make although they had spoken a bit over his head about their gourmet meals and their devotion to Gentleman's Relish. He found them taking a late lunch with a Big Value Pizza smothered in tomato sauce from a quart-sized plastic container. When he reported his News Flash across Exmoor it did nothing for their image that he pronounced pizza as 'pissa', describing it as 'one of they old pissa thingamijigs'.

If some neighbours seize on information to take away, others can also arrive bearing it, particularly children, who impart their gems matter-of-factly, as in 'Mother's gone to bed with the lodger and a bottle of gin.'

A phrase worth remembering might well be, 'Us can't come up to your level, so you'll have to come down to ours.' This is evidenced by the farmer who found his new neighbours' vehicle parked across his gateway. 'Do 'ee mind moving that truck?' he asked the wife. 'It is not a truck,' she replied icily. 'It is a Range Rover.' 'Like I said, m'dear,' answered the farmer. 'If you'd just be good enough to move yer truck ...'

t only takes seconds for little gaggles of countrymen to magic up out of the blue and become engrossed in deep conversation, leaning on their thumb-sticks and occasionally waving them to emphasise a point. The subject is unlikely to be world affairs. As one worthy succinctly phrased it: 'If it ain't happening up Hawkridge then I ain't concerned.'

Alternatively, nigh on Christmas, the charitable might construe the discussion to hinge on families and the purchase of gifts. Unlikely. Not one of the little congregation is ever likely to blow up a balloon, wrap a parcel, or even write a card. Christmas is not so much to be enjoyed as got through, the menfolk's main contributions being advice on how to run it and money (how not to spend it). Christmas is costly, and don't they know it. Farmer Fred blasts that it takes the best part of twelve months to rear half a sheep to pay for one bald-arsed turkey. Fred doesn't 'do' Christmas. The nearest he ever got to cards was glimpsing Missus scribble one off a pile a foot high 'To George and Nellie from Fred and Bertha.' Fred's mind drew blank on the recipients and, 'Who's Bertha?' he wanted to know. ''Tis me, you old fool,' trumpeted Mrs Fred indignantly. 'You'm right, Maid, so 'tis,' said her husband, remembering.

Another thing he remembered was to monitor Missus' wild spend-up at Christmas. Last year she announced she was sick of looking like one of her own pigs dressed in the same old red jumper and she took it into her head to splurge on a new Icelandic sweater. Farmer reckoned it cost near enough twenty quid, to which she nodded guiltily seeing he was about to have a seizure.

Calming down after a fairish sheep sale and a couple of whiskies, Fred thought he may have been a bit hasty with Missus and in a moment of totally alien madness decided to make amends by matching the sweater with another one. After all, Missus had been a fair enough maid over the years. A bit on the big side, but a proper worker.

Squaring his shoulders and pulling his cap over his ears he entered the local boutique and a different world, scented, and with music in the background, the floor space dotted with little satin covered chairs that a chap's arse would never fit square on. He wanted escape as a terrifying, beautiful, stick-thin vision approached him and he pointed, mute, to a pile of sweaters like the one Missus already had and slapped a twenty pound note on the counter.

'Excuse me, Sir,' purred the vision, 'but the Icelandics start at £56.'

With that Fred snapped back into his old self, grabbing his £20 back and heading for the door muttering that any gormless beggar that spent that much in a fancy shop wanted their head tested.

Mrs Fred wisely reverted to her old red jumper, indefinitely.

Men in Russia are said to deride any woman incapable of gutting a fish and most other countries seem to favour their own particular tests when it comes to their womenfolk coping with the inner man. Every man knows that Frenchmen demand a 'femme' who can cook up a tasty slab of horsemeat, whilst in Saudi Arabia perfectly cooked sheeps' eyes probably rate higher than the charms concealed under a Burkha, and in Cornwall a well-rounded Cornish pasty says it all.

Here on Exmoor, our menfolk effortlessly resist the temptations of foreign imports such as McDonalds or Pizza Parlour along with takeaways from the Big Bang, which, Farmer Fred decrees, sums up exactly what a chap who packs away a dodgy curry deserves. But none of it can hold a candle to the slimmest offering of the week, which is almost certainly one of Missus' Resurrection dinners, usually partaken of on a Monday, being Sunday's leftovers resurrected under varying guises. Farmer Fred and his fellow countrymen relate to their food in much the same way as an old collie buries his left-overs and digs them up the next day. A blip occurs if Missus is called away for a few days and it is a sad man who is left to manage his meals alone. Naturally, everything he could ever need is left fully prepared, but removing dinners from the freezer to the microwave is considered to be serious enough to invoke the cry – 'I'm left to do all me own cooking.' One wife, on a visit to her daughter abroad, left every meal ready for her farmer husband, plus some homemade soups, and then gave her man lessons on the microwave oven. He related to her over the telephone that although he managed to get the frozen soup hot, it never actually liquidised and he ate it with a knife and fork.

A few countrymen, carried away by their success at warming up their dinners, imagine they can actually improve on their womenfolk's cooking. One such would-be chef decided he fancied a jelly for his tea and dreamed up his own recipe for a gin jelly, selecting a lemon jelly and substituting hot gin instead of water. 'It tasted different,' was his reserved comment, but the crunch came later in the evening after a couple of pints of superphosphates in the pub when he admitted he 'felt a little bit funny, like.'

Generally, any food straying from the traditional is open to criticism. Farmer Fred shamed Missus at the Sheep Dinner from start to finish, ignoring dainty croutons and crumbling a large white roll into his soup, which then overflowed, but which he slurped with lip-smacking relish. Next came smoked mackerel which Farmer Fred scrutinised closely on his fork, then announced loudly: 'This fish be stone cold!' The lamb met with approval and he told the waitress: 'I'm all for a bit of mutton, Maid.' 'It's lamb, sir,' she replied. 'Don't you be fooled m'dear.' he told her, 'but if you likes to call ten-year-old sheep lamb, that's up to you, and no, m'dear, I won't hev no fishcakes with it.' 'These are croquette potatoes, sir, not fishcakes,' protested the waitress. Farmer Fred was not to be sidetracked. 'Now just you go back into thic kitchen m'dear and tell 'em, in these parts us hev roasted tetties with our mutton, not fishcakes, then they'll know for another time!'

The dessert was fresh fruit salad, which Farmer Fred pronounced tasteless — 'Tis better from a tin and none of it matches up to Missus' Resurrection dinner anyways.'

he latest must-have fashion this spring is hardly likely to coax farmers into rattling their money-boxes. The big-selling line is designer waistcoats sized in small, medium and large, and displaying the farm name. For chickens. In Japan the best looking hens were zipped into their little garments, and then they modelled on a catwalk. Farmer Fred thought this was a bit over the top, even for somebody like himself who is hardly on the same wavelength as Missus' poultry. He recalls defending himself in the hen run against a fiery cock-bird by snatching up a 3 x 2 plank of wood and knocking the bird unconscious. Half ashamed, and half fearful of Missus siding with the aggressor if she found out, he reached in his pocket for his hip flask, prised open the bird's beak and poured some of the fiery liquid down its throat. The effect was instantaneous, with the patient going straight for the jugular. Fred considered he had a lucky escape as he headed for safety, the battle reinforcing his longheld theory that there's only room for one cock in a hen run.

Chickens are big business worldwide, and no Wild West film is complete without a few hired hens scratching in the background. There is talk, howsoever, of an establishment in the deep south of America called the Chicken Ranch which has little to do with its name and everything to do with certain ladies whose work consists of taking hard-earned money off the local cow-pokes. An occasional raid from the police is countered with the girls rendering a rousing chorus of 'There ain't nobody here but us chickens', which the law indulgently smiles over. Songs about chickens are ever popular, from the pantomime dame clutching a plastic bird and screeching 'Altogether now – Hey little hen, when, when, when etc.' to the sad little ballad from the little

brown hen challenging the old red rooster with 'You don't come round as much as you use'ter.'

A bonus with poultry is that they are more easily handled than heftier farm stock. A father and son who farmed jointly for years had their lifestyle upset when the old man was taken ill and ordered to bed by their doctor. The son was dismayed at losing his right-hand man and inquired if father might do a little light work from his sick bed. The puzzled doctor agreed, but nothing too taxing, possibly form filling. On his next visit he found the old farmer propped up in bed on his pillows picking a chicken amid a cloud of feathers. 'Gimmee this little job any day,' he said. ''Tis a sight easier than form filling.'

Years agone, when eggs fetched a fair price, poultry injected a welcome sum into the household economy, in fact Missus was expected to keep house on her egg money, the rearing and maintenance of chickens being her sole department. According to the menfolk her life ran a parallel with her birds, commencing as a child or 'chick', progressing to a lively young pullet, then on to a little hen, followed by 'broody' with babies and, the final stage, a boiler, which was not a derogatory term as much as a fact of life.

If there's anything Farmer Fred hates more than the enemy in Missus' hen run it's the bantie cocks his new neighbour keeps. He threatens to kill them off and sell 'em back as pheasants, the only difference being the chap would have to sharpen his teeth.